CONTENTS

Moscow Mule Variations — 5
1. Classic Moscow Mule — 6
Adding Color to Your Mule — 7
2. Jalapeño Moscow Mule (Kicking Mule) — 8
3. Strawberry Moscow Mule — 10
4. Watermelon Mule — 12
5. Pineapple Moscow Mule — 14
6. Georgia Mule (Peach and Ginger) — 16
7. Holiday Mule — 18
8. Skinny Mule — 20
9. Hibiscus-Berry Mule Recipe — 21
10. Pomegranate Mule — 23
11. Mule Driver (Orange and Ginger Combo) — 25
Using Other Types of Alcohol — 27
12. Kentucky Bourbon Mule — 28
13. Dark and Stormy — 30
14. Gin Moscow Mule — 32
15. Moscow Mule Jello Shots — 34
16. Mexican Tequila Mule — 36
17. Garden Mule — 38
18. Mint Moscow Mule — 40

19. Blueberry Moscow Blue	42
20. Cherry Moscow Mule	44
21. Blood Orange and Pomegranate Syrup Moscow Mule	46
Conclusion	48
Unconventional Moscow Mule Recipes	49
Ready-to-Drink Moscow Mule Variations	50
Coming Up with Your Variations	51
Best Moscow Mule Recipes	52
Frequently Asked Questions (FAQs)	53

Moscow Mule – two words that in any language mean a great time. The basic Moscow Mule can seem simple or timeworn, but this drink is anything but boring. There are dozens of easy variations that will make this classic seem brand-new in just a few seconds. And none of them are much harder than the original recipe itself. Vodka, ginger beer, lime, enjoy!

Not Russian, and No Mule

So, what heavenly spirit gifted us this sweet and satisfying cocktail? According to adamant east coasters, the story goes like this. The year is 1941. The players are a vodka distributor, a ginger beer distributor, and a mysterious 3rd party. The setting is the Chatham Hotel, in New York's Little Moscow district, hence the name. At the time, ginger beer and vodka were both unpopular in the bar scene. The two distributors wondered if they could revitalize their product sales. They combined their products and, after a bit of experimentation, the Moscow Mule was born!

So, break out your copper mugs, find a ginger beer with a nice kick and try out these variations of the 21 best Moscow Mule variations.

MOSCOW MULE VARIATIONS

1. CLASSIC MOSCOW MULE

Ingredients

- 4-5 oz. Fever-Tree Ginger Beer
- 2 oz. Tito's Handmade Vodka
- ½ oz lime juice
- Fresh lime wheel for garnish

Instructions to make

1. Pour lime juice into a fresh chilled glass with ice (preferably a Moscow Mule pure copper mug, though a 10 - 11 oz highball glass will also work).
2. Pour in Tito's Handmade Vodka
3. Fill the rest of the glass with Fever-Tree Ginger Beer
4. Garnish with a lime wheel

ADDING COLOR TO YOUR MULE

The best part of classic cocktails is the endless opportunities for variation. You may not be able to teach an old dog new tricks, but you can certainly keep an old recipe from becoming an old hat! And with such a beautiful, well-balanced base, the Moscow Mule is primed for bolder flavors. Next time you've got friends over, wow them with your own craft cocktail flair!

2. JALAPEÑO MOSCOW MULE (KICKING MULE)

There's no better way to spice up a Moscow Mule recipe than with a little bit of spice. The jalapeño mule is great to beat the heat or bring a bit of tropical warmth to your midwinter hideaway. This variation adds the perfect hot-cool combination of mint and jalapeño to amplify the refreshing qualities of the original.

Ingredients

- 4 - 5 oz. ginger beer
- 2 oz. vodka
- ½ oz lime juice
- 1-2 jalapeño slices (to taste), seeds removed
- 1 sprig fresh mint
- Fresh lime wedge, a slice of jalapeño, and a mint leaf (for garnish)

Instructions to make

1. Using a muddler, smash lime juice, fresh mint, and jalapeño slices in the bottom of a mixing glass

2. Add vodka
3. Add ice and shake well
4. Strain the mixture juice into your chilled copper mug filled with ice
5. Pour ginger beer over the vodka mixture
6. Garnish with a lime wedge, jalapeño slice, and sprig of mint; or any combination of the three.

3. STRAWBERRY MOSCOW MULE

As a kid, the best part of summer was going out to pick-your-own strawberry patches with my family. We'd cart home boxes of the sweetest strawberries you could imagine. Now that I'm an adult, I like to mix this joyful summertime nostalgia with the best perk of being an adult: alcohol. Sweet strawberries set off the spiciness of the ginger beer which can be amplified with (if you dare) a sprinkle of black pepper.

Ingredients

- 4 - 5 oz. ginger beer
- 2 oz. vodka
- ½ oz lime juice
- 2-3 large fresh strawberries or 5-6 tiny ones, stems removed and sliced, 1 reserved for garnish
- 1 or 2 cranks of fresh black pepper (optional)

Instructions to make

1. Using a muddler, smash the strawberry slices with lime juice in a shaker tin

2. Add vodka
3. Add ice and shake well
4. Strain mixture into your chilled copper mug filled with ice
5. Pour ginger beer over the vodka mixture
6. Garnish with a strawberry
7. If you want to add a complex, grown-up touch, finish the drink off with a couple of cranks of fresh black pepper. This adds a great, deep flavor that brings out the slight sweetness of strawberries.

4. WATERMELON MULE

This drink is so pretty in pink it might make Elle Woods jealous. It's bright and festive. It's refreshing. And to top it off, all that watermelon means it's hydrating, so have as many as you want! (Or at least that's what I tell myself.) This variation really amps up the already cool, refreshing nature of the classic Mule.

Ingredients

- 4- 5 oz. ginger beer
- 1.5 oz. vodka
- 3 watermelon chunks
- ½ oz lime juice
- A sprig of mint for garnish
- Watermelon slice for garnish

Instructions to make

1. Muddle watermelon chunks and lime juice in a shaker tin
2. Add vodka

3. Add ice and shake well
4. Strain into a pure copper mug filled with ice
5. Pour ginger beer over vodka mixture until full
6. Garnish with a mint sprig and watermelon slice

5. PINEAPPLE MOSCOW MULE

Pineapples are about the most popular tropical fruits because not only it is delicious, it is also very healthy and versatile to use. It can be eaten raw, made into juices, jams, flavorings and others. The vodka-ginger beer-lime juice-pineapple juice combination is seriously refreshing, and a great choice of drink especially during the summertime.

Ingredients

- Ice
- 2oz vodka
- 2oz Dole 100% Pineapple Juice
- 1oz lime juice
- Zevia Mixer Ginger Beer

Instructions to make

1. Fill a copper mug with ice.
2. Add the vodka, pineapple juice, and lime juice.
3. Top with ginger beer and stir.
4. Garnish with a pineapple wedge, a ginger crystallized

candy and mint sprigs.

6. GEORGIA MULE (PEACH AND GINGER)

The reason ginger beer works so well for the Moscow Mule is that it has a nice fiery kick you just can't get with ginger ale. But sometimes even ginger beer isn't hot enough. When you find yourself longing for a southern-style combo of heat and sweet, this peach and ginger-enhanced Moscow Mule is perfect.

Ingredients

For the drink:

- 4 - 5 oz. ginger beer
- 1.5 oz. vodka
- 1 oz ginger-peach puree
- fresh peach slices for garnish
- candied ginger for garnish

For the ginger-peach puree:

- 2-3 large ripe peaches (with thin slices for garnish reserved) pitted and cut in half.
- 1 one-inch piece of fresh ginger (skin removed)

- ¼ cup lemon juice
- ¼ cup water
- 2 tbsp honey (more to taste if peaches are tart)

Instructions to make

1. Make the peach puree: Add all ingredients to your blender and puree until smooth. Taste and adjust flavors as needed (ginger for more heat, peaches, and honey for more sweetness, lemon juice for more sourness). Strain well using a fine strainer and discard all solids.
2. Add the ginger-peach puree and vodka into a cocktail shaker filled with ice & shake well
3. Strain the ginger-vodka mixture into a copper mug filled with ice
4. Pour ginger beer over the vodka mixture until the glass is full
5. Garnish with thin peach slices and candied ginger.

7. HOLIDAY MULE

Let this year be the end of heavy eggnog drinks and mulled wine's tyrannical reign over your office holiday party. For the holiday traditionalists among us, there's a middle ground so good it hardly feels like a compromise. Cranberry juice, rosemary, and ginger make a holiday spice that is more seasonally appropriate than you'd expect. Try them in these in the Holiday Mule.

Ingredients

- 1.5 oz. Tito's Handmade Vodka
- 2 oz. Ocean Spray Cranberry Juice
- Juice of 1 lime wedge
- Gosling's Ginger Beer (to top)
- Ice cubes
- Fresh or frozen cranberries (for garnish)
- Sprig of Rosemary (for garnish)

Instructions to make

1. Measure the vodka and cranberry juice with a jigger and pour them into a copper mug.

2. Fill the copper mug with ice cubes and squeeze the lime into it.
3. Top it off with ginger beer. Stir the drink with a bar spoon. Garnish with a handful of cranberries and rosemary.

8. SKINNY MULE

A Moscow Mule may be worth the calories, but sometimes we must give in to self-control. But when self-control is ready to live a little, there's a Mule for that, too. A low-sugar, low-calorie classic mule doesn't have to be the fantasy of your late-night cravings!

Ingredients

- 4 - 5 oz. Q Mixers Ginger Beer
- 1.5 oz. organic vodka
- ½ oz lime juice

Directions

1. Squeeze lime juice into a copper mug filled with ice
2. Add organic vodka
3. Fill the rest of the glass with ginger beer.
4. Garnish with a half lime wheel.

9. HIBISCUS-BERRY MULE RECIPE

Winter for me is long and full of dark beer. By the time spring has sprung I'm ready for anything fruity and floral. This bold, red variation has a floral sweetness that drives away the deepest of winter blues.

Ingredients

- 4 - 5 oz. Q Mixers Ginger Beer
- 1.5 oz. vodka
- ¾ oz Hibiscus-Berry Syrup
- ½ oz lime juice
- hibiscus flowers

For the hibiscus-berry syrup:

- 1 cup mixed berries, fresh or frozen (I used raspberries and blackberries)
- 1 cup hot water
- ¾ cup white sugar
- 4 Hibiscus-flavored tea bags or about ½ ounce dried hibiscus flowers

Directions

To make the Hibiscus-Berry Syrup:

1. Add hibiscus tea to hot water in a saucepan and steep for 5-10 minutes, until the color is a deep red
2. Remove hibiscus tea bags
3. Add remaining ingredients to a saucepan and mix well.
4. Bring to a gentle boil, stirring & using a fork to help break up the berries.
5. Once the mixture comes to a boil, turn to low heat for 5-10 minutes, stirring regularly until berries are completely integrated.
6. Cool to room temperature then strain into a glass container.

To make the cocktail:

1. Combine the hibiscus-berry syrup, lime juice, and vodka in a cocktail shaker filled with ice, shake well.
2. Strain the hibiscus-vodka mixture into a copper mug filled with ice
3. Pour ginger beer over the vodka mixture until the mug is full
4. Garnish with edible flowers.

10. POMEGRANATE MULE

If the floral notes of the hibiscus-berry mule aren't your style, try this pomegranate variation instead. It's just as bold and red but uses the tartness of pomegranate instead of floral hibiscus. This drink will make sure your friends don't take your bartending for pome-granted (I'll show myself out, hahaha!)

Ingredients

- 4 - 5 oz. ginger beer
- 1.5 oz. vodka
- ½ oz Pomegranate Juice (POM is a great alternative to fresh)
- ½ oz lime juice
- fresh pomegranate seeds for garnish
- lime wedge for garnish

Directions

1. Combine pomegranate juice, vodka & lime juice into a copper mug filled with ice

2. Pour ginger beer over the vodka mixture until the glass is full
3. Garnish with pomegranate seeds and a lime wedge.

11. MULE DRIVER (ORANGE AND GINGER COMBO)

This gingery cousin to the college-classic screwdriver is enough to drive away every bad memory you have of waking up hungover on a friend's couch when you were an undergrad. The orange and ginger combo is delicious and refreshing any time of day. And it may be tempting, but this doesn't mean you should pour yourself one of these for breakfast. Though if you do, I won't tell.

Ingredients

- 4 - 5 oz. ginger beer
- 1.5 oz. vodka
- 1 oz orange juice
- ½ oz lime juice
- Orange slice for garnish

Directions

1. Combine orange juice, vodka, and lime juice into a copper mug filled with ice
2. Pour ginger beer over the vodka mixture until the glass is full

3. Garnish with orange and lime slices.

USING OTHER TYPES OF ALCOHOL

The "ROYGBIV" method of cocktail variation is a great way to switch up your drink without having to stock a full bar. But why stop there? Adding new ingredients to a cocktail doesn't have to be the end-all of cocktail variations.

Switching up the liquor is a great way to transform the classic Mule into something new and exciting. Changing the liquor in your recipe allows you to get to the heart of the flavors that make a Moscow Mule delicious. You also can introduce a new depth to the drink. There are a few great classic vodka-free variations, some as popular as the Moscow Mule itself.

12. KENTUCKY BOURBON MULE

Nothing can make an all-American classic like the Moscow Mule more all-American or more classic than America's darling: bourbon! All true, great bourbons are born in Kentucky and bred from the finest American corn. Kentucky's passion for distilling has blessed us with the finest liquors in the world. A good Kentucky bourbon compliments ginger beer with vanilla notes and an extra-boozy kick.

Ingredients

- 4 - 5 oz. ginger beer
- 1.5 oz Kentucky bourbon
- ½ oz lime juice
- Mint sprigs for garnish

Directions

1. Combine bourbon and lime juice in a copper mug filled with ice

2. Top with ginger beer until the mug is full
3. Garnish with a lime wheel and mint sprig.

13. DARK AND STORMY

If the Moscow Mule wasn't familiar to you, you may recognize the name "Dark and Stormy." It's often billed on cocktail menus right beside its cousin. The Dark and Stormy is actually just another simple variation on the Moscow Mule.

The Dark and Stormy combines ginger beer with the equally-tropical flavor of rum. The rum adds a bit of sweetness to the cocktail and mellows out the bright flavors, opting for a darker finish. The Dark and Stormy is an excellent (and popular) tropical deviation from the Moscow Mule.

Ingredients

- 4 - 5 oz. Gosling's ginger beer
- 2 oz. Gosling's Black Seal Rum
- ½ oz lime juice
- Lime wedge for garnish

Directions

1. Combine rum and lime juice in a copper mug filled with

ice
2. Top the rum off with Reed's Ginger Beer until the glass is full
3. Garnish with a lime wedge.

14. GIN MOSCOW MULE

Vodka and gin are very similar, but juniper berries give gin its slightly floral flavor. Adding gin to a Moscow Mule adds a subtle herbal-floral note that is complemented by the ginger beer. I was skeptical the first time I had a gin mule.

I thought the ginger beer would overpower the subtleties of gin. But, if anything, it amplifies it in a very pleasant way! Try any of the different types of gin for unexpectedly exciting flavor combinations (I'm partial to Hendrick's cucumber notes and London dry gins).

Ingredients

- 0.5 oz simple syrup
- 0.5 oz lime juice
- 6-8 fresh mint leaves
- 1oz Q Drinks Spectacular Ginger Beer
- 2oz Tanqueray Gin

Directions

1. Gently muddle the mint leaves to release the oils.

2. Fill a beaker with ice, lime juice, gin and ginger beer.
3. Strain into a mule mug.
4. Garnish with spanked mint leaves.

15. MOSCOW MULE JELLO SHOTS

You always know a party is going to be great when you arrive and see a tray of neon jello shots making the rounds. Jello shots don't have to be the Kool-Aid flavored abominations of your younger years, though. This recipe for Moscow Mule jello shots elevates the fun party attitude of classic jello shots to something dare I say... classy? And it does it without sacrificing any of the fun or alcoholic punch of the original recipe.

Ingredients

- 8.5 oz ginger beer
- 1 ½ oz lime juice
- 2 envelopes (2 Tbsp) of unflavored gelatin
- 6 ounces of vodka
- nonstick cooking oil spray to easily remove from molds
- food coloring (optional)

Instructions

1. Combine ginger beer and lime juice (and food coloring) in a small pan
2. Sprinkle gelatin over the surface and allow it to rest 2 minutes as the gelatin activates
3. Warm the gelatin-ginger-beer mixture on medium-low heat for 2 minutes. Stir constantly and avoid allowing the mixture to boil.
4. Remove from heat and stir vodka into the mixture.
5. Spray molds with nonstick oil
6. Pour this liquid into the shot mold of your choice – ice cube trays, sample cups, mini-muffin tins, and sheet pans all work well
7. Refrigerate at least 4 hours, preferably overnight, until the shots are set completely
8. Remove jello shots from the mold by either sliding around the edges with a thin knife or cutting them into the desired shape (if using a sheet pan)
9. Keep the finished jello shots in the refrigerator and serve cold.

16. MEXICAN TEQUILA MULE

Much like the Kentucky Mule, this rendition of the Mexico Mule gets its name from the region's native inebriant. Tequila is made from the agave that is prevalent in Mexico, which has been harvested, crafted, and aged to create the signature liquor. As it turns out, tequila works quite nicely to mix up a Mule, and puts a refreshing twist on the traditional recipe. As always, the lime juice and high-quality ginger beer are the backbone of the drink but switch the vodka for some Camareña Family, Casamigos, Avion, or whatever brand you prefer.

Ingredients

- 1.5 fl oz Patron Reposado Tequila
- ¾ fl oz lime juice
- 1.4 fl oz simple syrup
- Ginger beer to top up
- Jalapeno slices
- Mint sprigs

- Lemon wheel

Instructions to make

1. Mix and shake tequila, lime juice and sugar syrup with ice.
2. Strain the mixture into an ice-filled glass.
3. Top it with ginger beer and stir.
4. Garnish with lemon wheel, jalapeno slices and mint sprigs and then serve.

17. GARDEN MULE

This jazzed-up version of the Mule calls for the vodka but also works well with gin or tequila. In addition to our friends, ginger beer, and lime juice, this interpretation of the Mule requires the addition of some flavor-enhancing accouterments.

Ingredients

- 4 slices cucumber
- 16 blueberries
- 6 mint leaves and sprig for garnish
- 2 ounces vodka
- 1 ounce lime juice
- ½ cup ginger beer
- 1 piece candied ginger

Instructions to make

1. Take a cocktail shaker and put cucumber, 8 blueberries

and mint leaves in the bottom
2. Muddle until the whole concoction is crushed and appears juicy
3. Add ice, lime juice, and vodka
4. Shake for 10-15 seconds
5. Put ice in the copper mug and strain the liquid into it.
6. Now, add ginger beer and 4 blueberries
7. Cut open the remaining 4 blueberries and candied ginger using a toothpick and use it alongside a sprig of mint.

18. MINT MOSCOW MULE

When you watch videos on how to make Moscow mules, the cocktail would be presented with a sprig of mint leaves acting as a garnish only. Sure, it adds to the aesthetics but the thing is, mint is such a powerful ingredient and it should be in the cocktail, not just a mere decoration. And yes, the ginger beer may already be the "kick" factor in the drink but sometimes, you kind of get used to it and perhaps you want something a little extra, and that's what the mint is for.

Ingredients

- 1.5 oz. Ketel One Vodka
- 6 - 8 mint leaves
- 1 whole fresh lime juice
- 1 C & H sugar cube
- 2 oz. Cock 'n Bull Ginger Beer
- Crushed Ice
- Sprig of mint leaves (for garnish)

Instructions to make

1. In a copper mug, put in the sugar cube, squeeze the lime with a citrus squeezer straight into the mug.
2. Muddle the combined ingredients gently for about 5 seconds. Add the mint leaves and give it two twists on the muddler.
3. Measure the vodka and ginger beer using a jigger and pour them into the copper mug.
4. Stir gently the contents using a bar spoon. Then, add in the crushed ice all the way to the top of the mug.
5. Finally, garnish it with a sprig of mint leaves.

19. BLUEBERRY MOSCOW BLUE

Last on our list is the Blueberry Moscow Blue. Instead of watermelon or strawberries, you will be using Blueberries. This one is a bit more complex than the other two. You have to prepare first the Blueberry shrub. It's advisable to make it ahead of time.

Ingredients

- ½ cup of water
- ½ cup of apple cider vinegar
- 1 cup of blueberries
- ¼ cup honey, agave, or simple syrup
- ½ teaspoon grated fresh ginger – this one is optional

Instructions to make

1. Take all these ingredients and put them in a blender. They should be fully liquified.
2. Pour mixture into a glass jar, and put in the refrigerator for at least 2 days.
3. Strain into a new and clean glass jar.
4. Once your blueberry shrub is ready. Put 1.5oz of vodka and the blueberry shrub into a shaker tin. Add some ice as well. Then, shake.
5. Use a strainer and pour the mixture into a barrel-style copper mug.
6. Top it with a ginger beer. Garnish it with blueberries and a lime wheel.

20. CHERRY MOSCOW MULE

Cherry Moscow Mule is a recipe that's made using Ginger ale and vodka which altogether is topped using some cherry juice and lime juice. If you are someone that likes less sweetness then you may use tart cherry juice. You can also use a regular beer as per what your palette demands.

Ingredients

- 6 Ounces Fever-tree Ginger Ale
- 6 Ounces Fever-Tree Ginger Beer
- 4 Ounces Vodka
- 2 Limes juiced, plus wedges for garnish
- 3 splashes cherry juice

Instructions to make

- Divide the ginger ale along with ginger beer

- Add some vodka in it and then mix with lime juice and cherry juice
- You can now serve it in 2 lowball glasses or copper mugs.
- Stir to combine
- Add ice and serve with lime wedges

21. BLOOD ORANGE AND POMEGRANATE SYRUP MOSCOW MULE

Blood Orange is a version of the Moscow Mule that has blood orange and pomegranate juice. You can garnish this mixture with sugar-coated cranberries and some rosemary. It is also considered as a fall wine or a festive cocktail.

Ingredients

- 1 Blood Orange
- 3 oz Vodka
- 2 cup pomegranate juice
- 1 (12oz) bottle of Fever-tree Ginger Ale

Instructions to make

- Take a cocktail shaker and combine all the juices.
- Shake them well.
- Distribute them evenly over copper mugs along with ice.
- Add some ginger beer over the mixture.
- Garnish with blood orange rosemary skewer.

CONCLUSION

And there you have it! It's not just a Moscow Mule, it's a Moscow workhorse! This simple and already hard-to-top cocktail has so many equally delicious variations it's hard to know where to start. So don't get caught up in the choices and just make time to try them all.

There is a variation for any occasion and the Moscow Mule, any flavor, is always refreshingly delicious. You'll never find yourself breaking a sweat with these easy and quick recipes. Sit back, relax, and take a trip to Moscow (or New York or LA, who's to say?).

UNCONVENTIONAL MOSCOW MULE RECIPES

With every experimentation and progress comes both excellent and unexpected outcomes-and that's especially true in creating cocktails. Listed below, for example, are some of the unique and absolutely fun twists on the classic Moscow Mule recipe that will surely surprise you!

- Fast Canoe - Ever heard of Pandan? It's a Southeast Asian tropical fruit, and delicious addition to the Moscow Mule recipe! Partnered with malt scotch whiskey Glenlivet, this dynamic duo might just be the unique Mule flavor that you're looking for.
- Chipotle Moscow Mule - A feisty take on the Mule, this version throws in chipotle, tequila, cilantro, and a bit of sugar to the original recipe.
- Icelandic Mule - Have you thought of adding apple cider to your Mule? Well, we're telling you right now, it's possible, and it has a great taste to it! Use apple cider to replace the lime juice and, with the help of simple syrup, this version of the Mule might just be legendary.
- Melon and Mint Mule - Watermelon is not the only pepo fruit that can add great flavor to the Mule. The melon liqueur Midori can be substituted to vodka, and adding a few mint leaves makes all the difference.

READY-TO-DRINK MOSCOW MULE VARIATIONS

Some of us can't always go to the bar or make their drinks at home. But that's not a problem! If you're craving for a refreshing sip of Moscow Mule, ready-made cans of Mule are now available and you can buy them in stores near you! Here are our top 10 choices of the best ready-to-drink Moscow Mule:

1. Moscow Mule 2.0
2. Smirnoff Moscow Mule Vodka
3. Gingerhead Moscow Mule
4. Salt Point Moscow Mule
5. Punching Mule Moscow Mule
6. The Copper Can Moscow Mule
7. Two Brothers Moscow Mule
8. Blue Marble Cocktails Moscow Mule
9. Russian Standard Moscow Mule Ready-to-Drink Cocktail
10. Joia Spirit Sparkling Moscow Mule
11. Moscow Mule with Whiskey

COMING UP WITH YOUR VARIATIONS

These variations are only some of the many possibilities that the delicious Moscow Mule can offer. Of course, you can make your variation too! Here are a few things to remember in making your recipe:

- **Take the original recipe as a reference.** The classic Moscow Mule is made of ginger beer, vodka, and lime juice, but you don't always have to use these ingredients. You may use their counterparts, for example, ginger ale can be used in the absence of ginger beer, and lemon juice can take the place of lime juice.
- **Don't be afraid to try other alcoholic drinks.** Sure, vodka works best for Mule especially since copper mugs enhance its flavor. But when people tried a different spirit and Bourbon came into the picture, the resulting variation-Bourbon Mule-became a great hit.
- **Bring flavor into your mule.** Watermelon, blueberries, strawberries, even hibiscus, and jalapeño. This list feature so many ingredients that bring out different flavors for you to try. Fruits are always good options but don't be afraid to try other components. Who knows, you might just create the next popular Mule recipe!

BEST MOSCOW MULE RECIPES

Every mug of Moscow Mule is uniquely satisfying. But, out of all the **Moscow Mule variations** listed above, there are a few that are exceptional in their ways. Specifically, they are the following:

Most Flavorful - Garden Mule

Most Popular - Bourbon Mule

Most Beautiful - Hibiscus-Berry Mule

FREQUENTLY ASKED QUESTIONS (FAQS)

Q: What alcohol is in a Moscow Mule?

The classic Moscow Mule recipe contains the distilled Russian alcohol, Vodka. This beverage interacts with copper and gives a better drinking experience, thus Moscow Mule is usually served in copper mugs.

Q: How do you make Moscow Mule without Ginger Beer?

In case you are craving for a refreshing mug of Moscow Mule but do not have Ginger Beer available, you can replace this drink with its counterpart, Ginger Ale.

Q: What is the difference between Ginger Beer and Ginger Ale?

Although both products are made from the same medicinal root- ginger, Ginger Ale is a non-alcoholic drink. Its health benefits make it a great cure for upset stomachs, vomiting, nausea, etc. and the absence of alcohol makes it appropriate for children to take. On the other hand, Ginger Beer may be alcoholic or non-alcoholic. It is stronger and more commonly used as an ingredient in cocktail recipes. Also, unlike the carbonated Ginger Ale, Ginger beer contains fermented yeast.

Q: What is the best Ginger Beer for Moscow Mule?

Fever-Tree Ginger Beer is an award-winning Ginger Beer that contains perfectly balanced natural ingredients. It is the ideal choice in mixing cocktails, especially for making Moscow Mule or its variations.

Q: Is Ginger beer in Moscow Mule alcoholic?

No. Ginger beer is not necessarily beer, but it still is a great addition to the Moscow Mule recipe since it pairs well with vodka, becomes fizzier because of the copper, and enhances the overall flavor of the cocktail.

Made in the USA
Middletown, DE
25 May 2022